LOBBYING:
A
CONSTITUTIONALLY
PROTECTED RIGHT

Hope Eastman

Hope Eastman is a partner in the Washington law firm of Charles Morgan, Jr., and Associates, Chartered.

ISBN 0-8447-3267-2

Library of Congress Catalog Card No. 77-85166

AEI studies 168

Printed in the United States of America

LOBBYING:
A
CONSTITUTIONALLY
PROTECTED RIGHT

American Enterprise Institute for Public Policy Research
Washington, D.C.

CONTENTS

1
INTRODUCTION

Although often portrayed as an evil influence on the legislative process, the lobbyist is exercising the constitutionally protected right to petition the government for redress of grievances.

The First Amendment confers broad immunity upon the activities of those who attempt to present their points of view to elected officials. As Chief Justice Charles Evans Hughes once wrote: "The maintenance of the opportunity for free political discussions to the end that government may be responsive to the will of the people and that changes may be obtained by lawful means, an opportunity essential to the security of the Republic, is a fundamental principle of our Constitutional system."[1] Further, as Mr. Justice Brennan once observed, "speech concerning public affairs is more than self-expression; it is the essence of self-government."[2]

The fact that the Constitution recognizes lobbying as a vital component of the democratic process does not mean that Congress is absolutely prevented from protecting itself and the public from corrupting influences. However, when it seeks to regulate constitutionally protected activity, Congress must demonstrate existence of a compelling and substantial governmental interest in doing so and then draw the legislation carefully and narrowly.

It is not the advocacy of ideas which gives lobbying a bad name. Vigorous advocacy is not corrupting. Rather, it is the favors which lobbyists can lavish on elected officials which raise suspicions in the mind of the public. It is no accident that the recently enacted congressional ethics rules focus on outside money as the chief corrupting

---

[1] Stromberg v. California, 283 U.S. 359, 369 (1931).
[2] Garrison v. Louisiana, 379 U.S. 69, 74-75 (1964).

influence. With an upper limit imposed on campaign contributions and with newly imposed limits on outside income of and gifts to members of Congress, the use of money by "special interests" to gain special ties to legislators will greatly diminish.

These recent changes in the federal election campaign laws and in the Senate and the House ethics codes have significantly lessened the governmental interest in lobbying disclosure legislation. In the final analysis, these remedies, not the disclosure of the advocacy features of lobbying, will purge corrupting influences from the government.

Comprehensive disclosure legislation is also comprehensive government monitoring of political activity, enforced by government subpoena power and criminal sanctions. Such a drastic proposal must be approached with great caution. Supporters of lobbying disclosure legislation often cite James Madison writing in *The Federalist*, Number 10. Quoting his alarmed description of the "factious spirit which has tainted our public administration,"[3] they never mention his very cautious solutions. Madison rejected both of the methods he perceived as the only ways to remove the causes of "faction"—"the one, by destroying the liberty which is essential to its existence; the other by giving to every citizen the same opinions, the same passions, and the same interests."[4] He turned to controlling its effects: "If a faction consists of less than a majority, relief is supplied by the republican principle, which enables the majority to defeat its sinister views by regular vote."[5]

The danger, according to Madison, was where the faction included a majority which could impose its will on the minority. Unlike a pure democracy, Madison argued, a republic, in its form of government alone, offers the cure: representative government and the large and diverse country encompassed by the republic which came to be the United States.

Madison's cures merit discussion because as we approach the question of government monitoring of those petitioning the government, as the Constitution contemplates, it is well to remember the checks and balances which already exist. In this way it will be possible to look more dispassionately at the evils of "faction" requiring control and to measure the effectiveness of the remedies against their adverse impact on the right of petition.

---

[3] *The Federalist*, Number 10.
[4] Ibid.
[5] Ibid.

2
THE RIGHT OF PETITION
AND THE RISE OF LOBBYING

The right of petition can be traced to the Magna Carta in 1215.[1] The early English parliaments were regular recipients of a wide variety of petitions.[2] As the English government became centralized and developed separate branches and agencies, fewer petitions were made to Parliament. But a residual right remained and came to be described by seventeenth century English judges as "the birthright of the subject."[3]

By the late eighteenth century the right of petition was flourishing in England and was used by the American colonists to express their grievances. In the Resolutions of the Stamp Act Congress, the colonists wrote in 1765: "That it is the right of the British subjects in these colonies to petition the king or either house of parliament."[4]

Similar language appeared in the resolves of the First Continental Congress.[5] The fact that "our repeated Petitions have been answered only by repeated injury" was one of the basic grievances of the Declaration of Independence.[6] And when the Bill of Rights was adopted in 1791, the First Amendment included the well-known words: "The Congress shall make no law . . . abridging . . . the right of the people

---

[1] Magna Carta, chapter 61 (1215) in Milton Viorst, *The Great Documents of Western Civilization* (New York: Chilton Books, 1965).

[2] William S. Holdsworth, *History of English Law* (London: Methuen and Co., 1908), pp. 172-73.

[3] *Encyclopedia of the Social Sciences*, vol. 12 (1934), s.v. "Petition, Right of."

[4] Richard L. Perry, *The Sources of our Liberties* (Chicago: American Bar Foundation, 1959), pp. 270-71, note 131.

[5] Ibid., pp. 286-88, note 131.

[6] William MacDonald, *Documentary Source Book of American History* (New York: McMillan Co., 1926), p. 194.

peaceably to assemble, and to petition the Government for redress of grievances."[7] As the Supreme Court would later describe it, "The very idea of a government, republican in form, implies a right on the part of its citizens to meet peaceably for consultation in respect to public affairs and to petition for redress of grievances."[8]

Lobbying is perhaps almost as old as the right of petition. As one commentator has described it, "Doubtless ever since representative assemblies began, citizens have visited them for purposes of persuasion."[9]

In the words of another:

> Lobbying in one form or another has been with us from the beginning. . . . It has, indeed, been so deeply woven into the American political fabric that one could, with considerable justice, assert that the history of lobbying comes close to being the history of American legislation.[10]

The great proliferation of organized groups engaged in lobbying has occurred in the twentieth century as the issues confronting government have become more and more complex.[11]

---

[7] U.S. Constitution, First Amendment.

[8] United States v. Cruikshank, 92 U.S. 542, 552 (1876).

[9] Robert Luce, *Legislative Assemblies* (New York: Houghton Mifflin, 1924), p. 367. Luce suggests that the beginning of professional lobbying in the United States began with Andrew Jackson's struggle with the United States Bank. However, lobbying, whether professional or not, appears even earlier. See *The Federalist*, Number 10.

[10] Edgar Lane, *Lobbying and the Law* (Berkeley and Los Angeles, Calif: University of California Press, 1964), p. 18.

[11] V. O. Key, Jr., *Politics, Parties, and Pressure Groups*, 5th ed. (New York: Thomas Crowell Company, 1964), p. 128. The chapter, "Roles and Techniques of Pressure Groups," pp. 128-61, contains an excellent short summary of the way organizations lobby Congress, administrators, the public, and each other.

3
CONGRESSIONAL EFFORTS TO REGULATE LOBBYING

Early Efforts

The efforts of Congress to regulate lobbying go back over 100 years when the House of Representatives first passed a resolution requiring all lobbyists to register with the clerk of the House.[1] In 1852, to protect itself from the "onslaught" of lobbyists posing as newspapermen, the House of Representatives barred from newsmen's seats on the floor anyone "employed as an agent to prosecute any claim pending before Congress."[2] In the mid 1930s, then Senator Hugo Black led a congressional investigation into lobbying by opponents of the New Deal's public utility holding company bill. It led to sensational disclosures but no legislation.[3]

It was not until 1946 that Congress enacted the first comprehensive law governing lobbying. That law, the Federal Regulation of Lobbying Act,[4] required that individuals and groups seeking to influence legislation in the Congress register with the secretary of the

---

[1] U.S. Congress, Senate, Committee on Government Operations, *Lobbying Disclosure Act of 1976,* S. Rept. 94-763, 94th Congress, 2nd session, April 26, 1976, p. 4. Edgar Lane traces the development of state lobbying statutes which during the second half of the nineteenth century were a response to the greed and dishonesty of the railroad builders and, later, to the excesses of those seeking charters and franchises from state governments. Lane, *Lobbying and the Law,* pp. 18-39.

[2] See *Congressional Globe,* 32nd Congress, 2nd session (1852); Comment, "Public Disclosure of Lobbyists' Activities," *Fordham Law Review,* vol. 38 (1970), p. 524, 526.

[3] Irving Dillard, *One Man's Stand for Freedom* (New York: Alfred Knopf, 1963), p. 14; Comment, *Fordham Law Review,* vol. 38, p. 528.

[4] Title III, Legislative Reorganization Act, 60 Stat. 812, 839 (1946).

Senate and the clerk of the House and file quarterly financial reports. It required registration of those paid to lobby for someone else if their "principal purpose" was to lobby. It was intended to cover both direct lobbying and efforts to stimulate grass-roots expressions of opinion on issues before the Congress.

Soon after its passage, its constitutionality was challenged on the grounds that it violated First Amendment guarantees of free speech, petition for redress of grievances, and free assembly. In 1954, while upholding the act's constitutionality, the Supreme Court, in *United States* v. *Harriss*,[5] significantly narrowed its reach to avoid having to find it unconstitutional, interpreting it to cover only lobbying efforts which involve direct contacts with a member of Congress.

Since 1954 there have been numerous congressional investigations and efforts to revise and expand the legislation regulating lobbying. None has resulted in legislative changes.[6]

Modern Efforts

In 1971, the House Committee on Standards of Official Conduct reported out the first comprehensive revision of the 1946 act. However, no action was taken on it by the full House. In the 94th Congress, in the wake of Watergate and other scandals, sweeping legislative changes were almost enacted into law.

In the Senate, the Government Operations Committee (now renamed Governmental Affairs) held five days of hearings on lobby reform proposals. In April 1976, it reported S.2477.[7] It was passed by the Senate on June 15 by an overwhelming vote.[8] Under that bill, an organization, but not an individual, would be a lobbyist if it (1) retained for at least $250 a quarter a law firm or other organization to lobby for it in Congress, (2) made twelve or more oral lobbying communications with Congress, or (3) spent $5,000 or more in a quarter on lobbying solicitations, in other words "grass-roots lobbying." The bill covered lobbying of the executive branch if it related to a measure before the Congress. Once the thresholds were met, detailed reporting requirements were triggered. The bill made enforce-

---

[5] 347 U.S. 612 (1954).

[6] Lobbying laws also exist in every state. Since 1972, more than half of the states have enacted such laws or amended old ones. U.S. Congress, House, Committee on the Judiciary, *Regulating Lobbying and Related Activities*, H. Rept. 94-1474, 94th Congress, 2nd session, September 2, 1976, p. 11.

[7] S. Rept. 94-763, April 26, 1976.

[8] *Congressional Record*, June 15, 1976, p. S9365.

ment the responsibility of the General Accounting Office, but litigation the responsibility of the Department of Justice.

In the 94th Congress, most of the lobbying bills in the House were jointly referred to the Judiciary Committee and the Committee on Standards of Official Conduct. In the first session of the 94th Congress, both committees held hearings, and on August 25, 1976, the Judiciary Committee reported H.R. 15.[9] Under H.R. 15, only an organization could qualify as a lobbyist. Such an organization would qualify in one of two ways: (1) if it spends more than $1,250 in any quarterly filing period to retain another person to make oral or written communications directed to a federal officer to influence legislation and certain executive agency decisions; or (2) if it employs at least one individual who spends 20 percent of his or her time in a quarterly filing period engaged on behalf of that organization in lobbying activities. The bill covered lobbying of executive agencies, but only of the highest-ranking executive officers. Like S.2477, the bill gave administrative and enforcement authority to the General Accounting Office, but Congress would have been granted specific powers to disapprove regulations issued pursuant to the act by the comptroller general.

On September 20, 1976, the House Committee on Standards of Official Conduct adopted an amendment in the nature of a substitute to H.R. 15.[10] That version had broader application than H.R. 15. Any organization employing someone who lobbies for six days in a six-month period would be covered. Like S. 2477, the bill would have used a separate threshold for groups that conduct only "grass-roots" lobbying efforts. The bill also eliminated the quarterly registration and reporting provision, requiring reports every six months instead. Additional registration information was also required, along with identification of officials, whether paid or not, who exerted a prominent role in the decision-making processes of the organization. Administration, enforcement, and civil and criminal sanctions were essentially similar to the Judiciary version of H.R. 15.

The full House took up the two lobby bills on September 28, 1976. By a roll-call vote of 291 to 74, the Standards Committee amendment in the nature of a substitute was defeated.[11] Early in the morning of September 29, after fourteen hours of debate, the House

---

[9] H. Rept. 94-1474, September 2, 1976.

[10] *Congressional Record*, September 20, 1976, p. H10612.

[11] *Congressional Record*, September 28, 1976, part 1, p. H11393-94.

passed the Judiciary Committee's version of H.R. 15, with additional amendments, by a roll-call vote of 307 to 34.[12]

H.R. 15 was then sent to the Senate, where it was referred to the Committee on Government Operations and thereby trapped by parliamentary procedure. Because of the Senate's intention to adjourn shortly for the year, bringing the bill from the committee to the floor for a vote required unanimous consent. Unable to get such unanimous consent, Senator Abraham Ribicoff (Democrat, Connecticut), chairman of the Government Operations Committee, conceded that the bill was dead for the year.

Bills in the 95th Congress

In the 95th Congress, the effort to enact lobbying legislation continued. Thus far, most of the activity has occurred in the House, with the Senate largely waiting to see what the House will do before it passes any bills.

Three major bills have been the focus of House attention in the Judiciary Committee. Recently, the Judiciary Committee's Subcommittee on Administrative Law and Governmental Relations reported H.R. 8494. Extensive consideration before the full Judiciary Committee is expected. The result of their deliberations, in all likelihood, will form the basis for any legislation passed by the House, although it is reasonable to assume that some of the major issues faced at the committee level will be reargued when the bill reaches the House floor.[13]

The Senate Governmental Affairs Committee held brief hearings on S. 1785 just prior to the introduction of S. 2026. S. 1785 utilizes a two-tier test to trigger the act's registration and reporting requirements. Any organization which makes fifteen oral lobbying communications in a quarter has to comply with one set of reporting requirements. Any group which (1) spends $1,250 to retain a lobbyist, (2) employs one or two people who spend twenty-four hours making or preparing oral or written lobbying communications, or (3) spends $5,000 in a quarter on lobbying solicitations must comply with a far more detailed set of reporting requirements.

---

[12] Ibid., part 2, p. H11416.

[13] The chances that Judiciary Committee action will in large measure determine the proposal which comes to the floor are enhanced by the fact that on January 4, 1977, the House voted to abolish the legislative jurisdiction of the House Committee on Standards of Official Conduct over lobbying disclosure legislation. U.S. Congress, House, H. Res. 5, 95th Congress, 1st session, *Congressional Record*, January 4, 1977, pp. 4–5.

S. 2026 uses a higher threshold to trigger any reporting requirement. It applies to any organization which in a quarter spends in excess of $2,500 to retain a lobbyist or spends $2,500 making lobbying communications *and* has one employee who averages eight hours per week making such communications.

The bill reported by the House Judiciary Subcommittee, H.R. 8494, would apply to any organization which spends $2,500 per quarter to retain a lobbyist to make lobbying communications or which (1) employs at least one person who "on all or part of each of thirteen days" in a quarter makes lobbying communications and (2) spends $2,500 on making such communications.

The three bills from which H.R. 8494 was drawn have a range of triggering levels similar to those in bills before the Senate. H.R. 5578, sponsored by Congressman Don Edwards (Democrat, California), applies to any organization which spends $2,500 per quarter on direct lobbying communications (including research and preparation) *and* either retains a lobbyist or employs one salaried employee who spends 20 percent of his or her time directly lobbying. The bill's sponsors seek to cover only those organizations which engage in significant lobbying activities and to exclude small, local organizations.[14]

H.R. 1180, introduced by Judiciary Chairman Peter Rodino (Democrat, New Jersey), resembles H.R. 15 as passed in 1976. The threshold for retained lobbyists is $1,250 per quarter. Although utilizing a threshold of 20 percent for employees, there is no salary level. Thus, an employee earning as little as $25 per week would trigger the bill. This would sweep in large numbers of small organizations doing even intermittent lobbying.

H.R. 5795, sponsored by Congressmen Robert Kastenmeier (Democrat, Wisconsin), and Tom Railsback (Republican, Illinois), uses a threshold for a retained person of $1,250 per quarter. For employees, the threshold is thirty hours per quarter for both direct communications *and* solicitations. Research and preparation time is not included.

The reporting requirements of the bills have been scaled down when compared with earlier versions, but still will involve organizations in much time-consuming record keeping and accounting.

The abbreviated lobbying report provision of S. 1785 requires

---

[14] Statement of Congressman Don Edwards (Democrat, California) before the Subcommittee on Administrative Law and Governmental Relations, House Committee on the Judiciary, April 4, 1976. See also the testimony of Kenneth Norwick and David Landau on behalf of the American Civil Liberties Union before the same subcommittee, April 6, 1977.

an organization to report all gifts to or on behalf of members of Congress, expenditures of over $500 for dinners or receptions for federal officers, and a description of its ten major issues. This provision requires a description of written lobbying solicitation efforts which might reach 500 or more people, 25 directors, 100 employees, or 12 affiliates, including an indication of the size of the audience reached by mail and a detailed listing of any advertisements. The full lobbying reports provision of S. 1785 requires reporting of the following: the approximate amount of total expenditures for lobbying communications and for lobbying solicitations; the names of paid officers, directors, and employees who lobby in excess of twelve hours in a quarter; the names of and amounts paid to any retained lobbyists; a description of the thirty major issues on which the organization lobbied, along with the names of the lobbyists and any chief executive or principal operating officer who lobbied on each issue; and, with respect to lobbying solicitations, approximately the same information required on the abbreviated form. Under H.R. 8494 each organization must report its total lobbying expenditures, itemizing only gifts over thirty-five dollars made to or on behalf of members of Congress. It must report salaries or other amounts paid to lobbyists and identify the major issues on which it lobbied.

H.R. 5578 contains two significant differences from these bills. As the bill requires no reporting of solicitations there is no need to create elaborate systems for decentralized organizations. Nonprofit groups under Section 501 (c) (3) of the Internal Revenue Codes will be able to file their Internal Revenue Service reports in lieu of the report on expenditures.[15]

The bills also vary in their requirements for disclosure of contributors. S. 1785 requires disclosure of contributors of above $3,000 to any organization which spends 1 percent of its budget on lobbying.

---

[15] Organizations which are tax-exempt under Section 501 (c) (3) of the Internal Revenue Codes have a special problem. Under that section, organizations which devote a "substantial" part of their activities to lobbying can lose their tax-exempt status. Section 1307 of the 1976 Tax Reform Act, 90 Stat. 1720, 26 U.S.C. 501, quantified the amounts they can spend and created elaborate reporting requirements. If a new lobbying statute requires them to file a report based on a broader definition of lobbying, they fear the government will use that other information to attack their tax report, thus recreating the uncertain threat to their tax status which the Tax Reform Act sought to end. Justice Department testimony before the House and Senate in 1975 strongly opposing a provision which would have barred the government from using lobbying reports in just this way suggests that their fears are very real. Senate Hearings, May 15, 1975, pp. 347-48; House Hearings, September 12, 1975, pp. 680-81. Only H.R. 5578 deals adequately with this problem by letting 501 (c) (3) groups file the same reports under any new statute which they file under Section 1307.

H.R. 8494 contains no contribution-disclosure requirement. S. 2026 and H.R. 5578 require no such disclosure and expressly bar the comptroller general from access to "any membership or contributor list of any voluntary membership organization." H.R. 5795 requires the disclosure of all the names of any individuals or organizations contributing more than $3,000. A person fearing harassment from disclosure can petition the comptroller general to stop public disclosure, but can only stop disclosure to the government itself if his or her contribution is under 5 percent of the organization's income. H.R. 1180 requires disclosure of the names of contributors of over $2,500.

All of the bills vest enforcement in the comptroller general and give him broad subpoena powers. H.R. 5578 authorizes the comptroller general to require maintenance of only records "essential" to compliance. However, all of the bills broadly authorize the comptroller general to obtain any "reports, records, correspondence, and answers to questions" which he "may consider necessary" for enforcement.

These bills thus present the major issues which need to be analyzed before we can determine whether there is any room—consistent with the First Amendment—for regulation of lobbying the Congress.[16]

---

[16] H.R. 1180 and H.R. 5795 both cover lobbying of the executive branch. Neither covers lobbying by executive branch officials. H.R. 5578 does not cover lobbying of the executive branch and includes federal and state lobbying of the Congress. There seems to be no basis for excluding from the bill lobbying of the Congress by executive branch officials who are, after all, major influences on the legislative process. Similarly, despite a contrary decision in Bradley v. Saxbe, 338 F.Supp. 53 (D.D.C. 1974), the Justice Department believes that a constitutional provision covering lobbying by state and local officials can be drafted. U.S. Congress, House, *Hearings on Public Disclosure of Lobbying Act*, September 12, 1975, pp. 667-68.

Lobbying of executive branch officials seems to present a whole range of complex issues which have not been adequately explored by the Congress and which, therefore, ought to be treated in a separate bill. Commentators agree with this conclusion. See, for example, Committee on Administrative Law and Committee on Federal Legislation, *Lobbying Disclosure Act of 1976* (New York: Association of the Bar of the City of New York, May 28, 1976).

4

CONSTITUTIONAL
CONSIDERATIONS

Basic First Amendment Test

Many practices which could be included under the rubric of lobbying have, of course, long been banned by federal laws on bribery[1] and buying influence.[2] The congressional proposals now under consideration do not directly restrict or prohibit any lobbying activity.[3] Their method of regulation is disclosure, with enforcement by subpoena power, fines, and criminal penalties. In this way the government becomes a monitor of those exercising their right to petition guaranteed by the First Amendment.[4]

Government actions to monitor the right to petition conflict with the First Amendment. The latest Supreme Court articulation of the

---

[1] 18 U.S.C. §201.

[2] 18 U.S.C. §203.

[3] Some state legislatures have in the past done just that. In Georgia, for example, the state constitution in 1877 provided that "lobbying is declared to be a crime." Georgia Constitution art. I, §2-205 (1945). Other state laws more specifically prohibited the "bribery and graft" aspects of lobbying. See Comment, *Fordham Law Review*, vol. 38, p. 526.

[4] The legislation before Congress treats individuals and corporations alike for purposes of analyzing the application of the First Amendment to lobbying. In Eastern R.R. Presidents' Conference v. Noerr Motor Freight, Inc., 365 U.S. 127 (1961), the Supreme Court held the Sherman Act inapplicable to a combination of large railroads which had united to conduct a campaign for regulation to restrict the trucking industry. The court suggested a contrary result would raise First Amendment questions. See also United Mine Workers v. Pennington, 381 U.S. 657 (1965). However, questions have been raised as to whether corporations have First Amendment rights. Commentators have questioned the view that corporations are included within the concept of "people" to whom the First Amendment guaranteed the right to petition. See, for example, "Lobbying and Antitrust," *UCLA Law Review*, vol. 14 (August 1967), p. 1211.

test against which such efforts must be measured is in *Buckley* v. *Valeo*.[5] Although an even stiffer test should perhaps be used, the *Buckley* test is a demanding one:

> We long have recognized that significant encroachments on First Amendment rights of the sort that compelled disclosure imposes cannot be justified by a mere showing of some legitimate governmental interest. Since *Alabama* [*NAACP* v. *Alabama*, 357 U.S. 449 (1958)] we have required that the subordinating interest of the State must survive exacting scrutiny. We also have insisted that there be a "relevant correlation" or "substantial relation" between the governmental interest and the information required to be disclosed.[6]

The two-part test demands not only a legitimate governmental interest for seeking disclosure but also a "subordinating" one which must survive "exacting scrutiny" on First Amendment grounds. Moreover, the disclosure must be closely correlated with the subordinating interest and have a substantial relationship to it.

If, for example, a piece of legislation is aimed at preventing bribery, it cannot under this First Amendment test require that an organization submit copies of its publications because there is not a sufficient correlation or relationship between the evil of bribery and disclosure of publications an organization has issued. Thus, the articulation of a subordinating governmental interest for lobbying disclosure legislation is essential not only for drafting a constitutional statute but also for determining its scope.

Goals of Legislation

What, then, is the "subordinating" need for this legislation? At the outset, it is necessary to deal with the image of the lobbyist which greatly influences the drive for regulation. This image unquestionably fuels the demand for lobbying-reform legislation in this post-Watergate era.

The traditional view of the lobbyist is a negative one—a man with a suitcase full of money. The comments of Senator Charles Percy (Republican, Illinois) in Senate lobbying hearings in 1975 are still typical and oft repeated:

> Many times when young children are down here . . . I get a lot of questions on "What is a lobbyist?" It almost has a

---

[5] 424 U.S. 1 (1976).

[6] Ibid., p. 64. Footnotes omitted.

sinister connotation, such as a connotation that is put on a person when he is called a politician rather than a statesman.[7]

As Edgar Lane described so well, in the nineteenth and early twentieth century the picture was an apt one.[8] There can be no doubt that lobbyists have used money to buy access more recently as well.[9]

Federal law has long prohibited the most glaring of such activities. The major twentieth century loophole—campaign finance—which provided the lobbyist with a special weapon has been significantly reduced by the enactment of the 1974 amendments to the Federal Election Campaign Act.[10] This act limits the amounts individuals can give, requires disclosure by the candidate of contributions received, and improves the regulation of political action committees set up by corporations and unions. The longstanding prohibitions on direct contributions and independent expenditures by corporations and unions continue.[11] The number of post-Watergate prosecutions and convictions for violations of these laws should make them a far more effective deterrent than in the past. Recent passage in both the Senate and the House of ethics rules, which limit both outside earned income and direct gifts and require disclosure, have closed the last loophole.[12]

If these negative aspects of lobbying have been dealt with by statutes and rules, what does this legislation seek to correct?

In recent testimony before the House Judiciary Committee's Subcommittee on Administrative Law and Governmental Relations, a representative of Common Cause, the chief proponent of lobbying

---

[7] U.S. Congress, Senate, Committee on Governmental Operations, *Hearings on Lobbying Reform Legislation*, April 22, 1975, p. 4.

[8] Lane, *Lobbying and the Law*, pp. 19-39.

[9] Drew Pearson and Jack Anderson, *The Case against Congress* (New York: Simon and Schuster, 1968) pp. 295-408.

[10] 2 U.S.C. §431 *et seq.*

[11] 2 U.S.C. §441b.

[12] On April 1, 1977, the Senate passed S. Res. 110, Official Conduct Amendments of 1977, which, among other provisions, (1) required senators, senior Senate employees, and candidates for the Senate to file detailed financial statements to be available to the public, (2) barred gifts over $100 from any "person, organization, or corporation having a direct interest in legislation" or from a foreign national, (3) limited senatorial honoraria to $1,000, (4) placed a 15 percent limit on outside earned income, and (5) barred senators and staff from certain lobbying for one year after leaving the Senate. On March 2, 1977, the House passed similar legislation, H. Res. 287. Its relevant provisions include (1) a prohibition on gifts over $100 from persons "having a direct interest in legislation" or from foreign nationals, (2) a 15 percent limit on outside earned income, and (3) a $750 ceiling on an individual honorarium.

disclosure legislation, argued for a new federal lobbying law. Companies were said to have spent large sums of money to lobby, sums not disclosed under existing lobbying laws, presumably because lobbying is not a "principal purpose" of the companies.[13]

In earlier testimony in the Senate, Common Cause Chairman John Gardner described lobbying as "one of the most secretive and potentially corrupting ingredients in American politics."[14] The examples he cited reflect the existing loopholes in the lobbying law:

- the American Trial Lawyers using Western Union to solicit mailgrams opposing no-fault insurance;[15]

- ITT using high level personal contacts in the White House and in the executive departments to persuade the Department of Justice to drops its antitrust suit;[16]

- the American Electric Power Company conducting a $3.6 million advertising campaign in 260 national and local publications, some calling for legislative change.

None was a registered lobbyist.

The senators listening to this testimony expressed similar concerns. Senator Ribicoff:

But to protect the democratic process itself, and assure public confidence in it, the lobbyist must work in the open. His

---

[13] Testimony of Fred Wertheimer, vice president, Common Cause, before Subcommittee on Administrative Law and Governmental Relations, House Committee on the Judiciary, April 6, 1977. His testimony contained two specific examples: AT&T spending over $1 million lobbying for a major communications bill and El Paso Natural Gas disclosing to the FPC the expenditure of almost $900,000 lobbying on a bill concerning divestiture of a pipeline. Neither was reported under the lobbying law.

[14] Statement of John Gardner, chairman, Common Cause, Senate *Hearings on Lobbying Reform Legislation*, April 22, 1975, p. 44-47.

[15] See discussion of grass-roots lobbying below at p. 23. The implications drawn by advocates of a new lobbying law—that communications to Congress are less reliable if solicited by someone else—is not valid. Where, as in the American Trial Lawyers example, telegrams were sent in the names of persons who had not authorized them, a far less drastic solution in terms of its impact on First Amendment freedoms is imposition of some requirement on Western Union to prevent fraudulent use of the names of third parties.

[16] See discussion of executive-branch lobbying above at p. 11, footnote 16. Early in the 94th Congress, proponents of this legislation were looking for ways to "smoke out" and require disclosure of any last minute contacts on congressional legislation. These efforts have been abandoned, in the recognition that the only way to accomplish it—requiring lobbyists to report every visit to government officials—was far too burdensome and inconsistent with the First Amendment.

work must not be cloaked in secrecy. Secrecy inevitably spreads public suspicion. Secrecy helps disguise the voice of a single special interest as the voice of the general public . . . the stream of letters or mailgrams we all receive may be a spontaneous reflection of the public view, or it may only represent a secretly-generated campaign by just one special interest. Congress and the public have a right to know which it is.[17]

Senator Percy said:

[Lobbying] remains shrouded in a veil of secrecy. . . . These legislative proposals have one simple purpose—to bring these activities out into the open.[18]

Senator William Brock (Republican, Tennessee) asked:

Can we, as individuals entrusted with decision making powers, accurately assess the goals and needs for legislation without knowing the source of the information and opinions we receive?[19]

And Senator Edward M. Kennedy (Democrat, Massachusetts) said:

Day after day armies of lobbyists patrol the corridors of Congress and every Federal agency. Vast amounts of influence and money are spent in secret ways for secret purposes, and many private interests are rich and powerful, and their secret operations corrupt the public interest.

The time has come to end that undue influence over the executive branch and really over the Congress. And too often we have allowed the voice of the people to be silenced by a special interest group clamoring for favored treatment.[20]

The common elements which run through most of these statements are secrecy and the expenditure of vast sums of money. Virtually all of the reformers' charges involve enormous amounts of money spent to stimulate grass-roots communications to Congress, huge advertising and public relations campaigns, and the use of "armies of

---

[17] Senate *Hearings on Lobbying Reform Legislation*, April 22, 1975, p. 1.

[18] Ibid., pp. 2-3.

[19] Ibid., p. 5. Senator Brock cited two additional examples of massive public relations campaigns which went unreported under the 1946 law: a "million dollar public relations campaign in support of the Surface Transportation Act" by the Association of American Railroads and the unreported expenditure of $839,892 in 1971 by El Paso Natural Gas "for the purpose of influencing public opinion."

[20] Ibid., p. 8.

lobbyists." Senator Kennedy perhaps expressed it best: "Vast amounts of money and influence are spent in secret ways for secret purposes." There is a sometimes expressed, but often implicit, wish to give the less well-financed groups an equal shot at influence. And because there is no easy way for the public to find out about these activities, sinister motives are often ascribed to them.

At this point it is vital to reiterate what kind of secret expenditure of vast sums we are talking about in the context of these lobbying laws. It is not bribes. It is not campaign contributions. It is not the provision of election-year manpower. It is no longer even expensive lunches, dinners, and other direct gifts.

Lobbying laws are aimed elsewhere. Congress seeks disclosure of groups spending money to send people to talk to members of Congress and other government officials, institutions communicating information to citizens—by direct solicitation or by indirect advertising campaigns—in order to get them to communicate their views to those government officials.

Performing those functions, organizations which lobby are playing a valuable role in the political process:

> [L]obbyists do on many occasions perform extremely useful functions in the national interest. They can be tapped for expert information on problems, they can analyze the impact of proposed legislation on their areas of concern, and they are an effective vehicle for representation of the interest group they represent.[21]

These, then, are the asserted interests in promoting lobbying reform. Are they sufficiently compelling to justify the impact on constitutionally protected activities, and under what circumstances?

Thresholds and Reporting

Feared Impact. Although the legislation is aimed at focusing public attention on well-financed lobbying efforts, the bills before Congress sweep within the ambit of regulation far more than the major sources of influence in Congress. To assess the impact on the right to petition, it is necessary to look at the thresholds used by the bills to trigger the registration and reporting requirements. These thresholds may be too low or the reporting burdens may be too heavy on those whose activities are too small to be accused of seeking an unfair advantage. If so, the Congress will have gone too far.

---

[21] Senator Percy in ibid., p. 3.

As a witness for Public Citizen, a Washington-based lobbying group, told a recent congressional hearing:

> A poorly designed and drafted version of lobbying disclosure could, however, have a major chilling effect on the exercise by some people of their right to petition the government. As the Supreme Court told us in United States v. Harriss, 347 U.S. 612 (1954), lobbying disclosure directly affects First Amendment rights. Thus, certain organizations which would otherwise communicate with Congress about an issue would not do so if they had to comply with the lengthy disclosure requirements of the proposed lobbying bills. These organizations would opt out of the political process for any of a number of reasons: the cost of compliance; the stigma of being labeled a lobbyist; the fear of government meddling in the organization's affairs; the assessment by the organization that the benefit of contacting Washington might be outweighed by the burdens of complying with the registration and reporting requirements. The organizations which are likely to cease communicating with Washington are not the organizations which have testified before you. Public Citizen, Common Cause, the AFL-CIO, the Chamber of Commerce, and the National Association of Manufacturers will all continue to lobby. The organizations which will opt out if they are covered are small business, local labor unions and grass roots citizen organizations. . . .
>
> The Congress, therefore, has a choice. It can write a bill which seeks to disclose every attempt to influence legislation at the risk of freezing some organizations out of the legislative process. Or it can write a bill which will disclose the lobbying efforts of the organizations which spend significant effort and money on lobbying while protecting the constitutional rights of all who would like their voice heard in Washington. Because we are dealing with First Amendment rights, we firmly believe that the Congress, if it must err, should err on the side of under-inclusiveness and not on the side of over-inclusiveness.[22]

These sentiments have been echoed by a wide range of interest groups—the Wilderness Society, the Chamber of Commerce, the National Association of Manufacturers, the AFL-CIO, the American Civil Liberties Union, the American Legion. The deterrent effect of the bills before Congress predicted by these groups for smaller, less-

---

[22] Testimony of Andrew A. Feinstein, Public Citizen, before the Subcommittee on Administrative Law and Governmental Relations, House Committee on the Judiciary, April 29, 1977.

19

organized groups, if not for themselves, has generally been dismissed by members of Congress as merely the self-protective cries of lobbyists.[23] By and large their fears have been discounted.

The California Experience. Now there is evidence from a source other than the interest groups themselves. In 1974, Californians enacted the Political Reform Act of 1974.[24] It was overwhelmingly approved by the voters of the state in an initiative known as Proposition 9. Like the bills before Congress, it was viewed as the remedy for too much money in politics and as the way to equalize access to legislators and politicians. Like the bills before Congress, it defines lobbying broadly to include direct and indirect attempts to influence legislation. The expenditure of $250 in any month by any person, business, or organization constitutes lobbying and must be reported. For an employee to become a lobbyist, lobbying must be a "substantial and regular" part of his or her duties. Gifts to politicians above $10 a month are prohibited. Lobbyists were also to be prohibited from "arranging for" political contributions, but that provision was overturned by a California court.[25]

In April 1977, the Political Reform Project of the Center for Ethics and Social Policy in Berkeley, California, released a brief study which examined the impact of the act in actual practice. In the author's words, "The test of any piece of legislation, of course, is to be found in an examination of its consequences and not in the intentions of its drafters."[26]

His findings confirm the fears of the witnesses who have urged caution on the Congress:

---

[23] See, for example, the exchange between Andrew Biemiller, director of the Department of Legislation of the AFL-CIO and Congresswoman Barbara Jordan during House Judiciary Committee hearings on lobbying reform. U.S. Congress, Subcommittee on Intergovernmental Relations, House Committee on the Judiciary, *Hearings on Regulation of Lobbying and Related Activities,* 94th Congress, 1st session, September 23, 1975, pp. 928-32. Indeed some members of Congress have refused to speak to any lobbying group about these bills.

[24] Title IX, California Government Code; §§81000-91014.

[25] Institute of Government Advocates v. Younger, L.A. Superior Court, No. C-110052, November 18, 1975. In evaluating the bills before Congress, it is interesting to note that the proponents of the California law considered this a crucial check on the power of lobbyists because it provided a way to break the link between lobbying and campaigning.

[26] Arthur Lipow, "Political Reform and the Regulation of Lobbying: The California Experience after Two Years," unpublished paper, April 1977. See also Lipow, "Political Reform as a Danger to Democracy," *California Journal,* August 1975, p. 267.

The result has been a blizzard of paper, a flurry of press releases from the Commission and, after some initial interest in the not surprising news that powerful and wealthy groups gave money to politicians (frequently on both sides) and spent money to influence legislation, there was a rather disenchanted yawn from the public.

Indeed, it would seem that the greatest burden of the law has fallen on the groups who were most adamant in their support of the law—the so-called "public interest" lobbyists and the representatives of the various non-profit charitable groups.[27]

Lipow quotes Allen Tebbetts, a lobbyist: "The great irony of all," according to Tebbetts, "is that the 'endangered species' is not the lobbyists per se, but the so-called 'good-guy' lobbyists, the ones without the bankroll."[28]

He quotes Secretary of State March Fong Eu:

With all due respect to the initiative's sponsors and proponents and with all due respect to the assumptions which have no doubt governed their thoughts, the bottom line to date (the end of 1975) is that the big fish are getting away and an awful lot of little fish are going to be caught.[29]

Further, according to Lipow, many of the public interest lobbying groups which strongly endorsed passage of Proposition 9 now "wish they had never heard of it."[30]

Measuring the Congressional Proposals

The California experience leaves no doubt that the fears of many that a comprehensive lobbying disclosure statute would fall most heavily on smaller, less well-financed groups and thus inhibit, impede, and indeed deter their participation in the legislative process were well-founded. If that is the predictable effect, the First Amend-

---

[27] Ibid., p. 3. He reports as well that one small labor union spends at least three to four days a month keeping records and filing reports and that the Franchise Tax Board is requiring full yearly audits. In one such case (see footnote 63 below) the board has subpoenaed a collection of documents which will be extraordinarily time-consuming to prepare.

[28] Ibid., p. 4. The one factor, according to Lipow, that has made life more difficult for "contract lobbyists, is the strict limit on entertainment expenses." Interestingly enough, he finds that what he describes as "major corporate and financial interest" lobbyists did little "wining and dining" in Sacramento.

[29] Ibid., p. 12.

[30] Ibid., p. 12.

ment requires that it be avoided unless the statute's supporters can show a "subordinating" interest. In light of the articulated reasons of the sponsors—"vast amounts of influence and money are spent in secret ways for secret purposes"—then it seems that, at a minimum, that test can be met only if Congress focuses on the most significant lobbying groups, measured in terms of money spent on any given issue, and lets all the rest go unregulated.

None of the bills before the Congress meets this standard. One requires the expenditure of $1,250 a quarter, another $2,500. A third would be triggered by a single $5,000 newspaper ad.

Under S. 1785, any organization's employment of even one person who spends twenty-four hours in a quarter preparing for or making oral or written lobbying communications triggers the bill's requirements. Organizations of all sizes are covered. The abbreviated reporting requirements would be triggered by an even smaller lobbying effort. For example, a group of housewives might organize to encourage the arts in their community. One housewife volunteer coordinates the group's activities at a nominal salary of twenty-five dollars per week. During the consideration of a single bill before Congress, she organizes a letter-writing campaign, devoting her full time to it for about four weeks. The group would then be a lobbying organization and would face fines and criminal penalties unless it registered as a lobbyist.

A threshold based on lobbying "all or part of each of thirteen days," as in H.R. 8494, even when coupled with a required expenditure of $2,500, would be too low. If an organization wanted to communicate with the Committee on the Judiciary regarding a single piece of legislation or a single issue, it would first have to devise an elaborate reporting and record-keeping scheme to comply with the complex and burdensome reporting provisions.

These thresholds would sweep within the statute many small local organizations, with little money and already overburdened staffs, as well as large, loosely organized national grass-roots organizations. For them, compliance would be extremely burdensome. Extensive records and intricate accounting and internal reporting procedures would be necessary to prove compliance. Record-keeping would have to be centralized, and expenditures on lobbying solicitations would have to be tracked as they filter through and multiply at various levels of the grass-roots organizational structure. This process would be too intimidating and too costly for many organizations. The threat of criminal sanctions is especially intimidating to small or inexperienced groups venturing into lobbying. Too many citizens—

especially those who have never had an adequate voice—would be deterred from organizing to enter the legislative arena at all.

The low level of these thresholds, coupled with the burdens of compliance and the presence of criminal sanctions, will deter many groups and individuals from even entering the lobbying process. Congress will thus have caused citizens to forsake their constitutionally guaranteed right to petition the government for redress of grievances. Where such a deterrent effect on First Amendment activity is possible and, indeed, predictable, legislation cannot survive the "exacting scrutiny" required by the First Amendment.

Regulation of many of the groups which would be covered by most of the proposals before Congress bears no relation to the prevention of corruption in government. Their efforts are intermittent; their impact on the legislative process is often slight and their activities are open to public view.

In drafting the First Amendment, the founding fathers sought to protect the ability of citizens to band together to petition their government. Historically, public educational campaigns, which in part ask people to write to Congress, have been the key to the major social reform movements in this country—from the American Revolution through the abolitionist and the civil rights movements, to the demand for impeachment after Watergate. Such movements have begun small and gradually snowballed into forces for social change. The guarantees of the First Amendment have given these citizens' movements breathing space in which to grow.

"Grass-Roots" Solicitation

Some of the proposals before the Congress would require registration and disclosure only by organizations which engage in direct contacts with members of Congress and congressional employees. In contrast, the requirements of other proposals are also triggered by engaging in activities known generically as lobbying solicitations. Others, while employing only direct contacts as the threshold, require reporting of such "lobbying solicitations."

While the definitions vary somewhat, lobbying solicitations typically include the efforts by organizations to require, encourage, or solicit like-minded citizens to make direct contacts with members of Congress or their staffs. Under some of the proposals, organizations which never contact members of Congress, but only try to affect legislation through appeals to the public, will be swept within the lobbying statute.

The regulation of such lobbying solicitations would bring virtually all activity designed to promote a given public policy viewpoint—all information dissemination, all expression of opinion, all attempts at persuasion—within the purview of a lobbying disclosure statute.

Under the *Buckley* standard, only where the expenditure is so large that the public would draw some negative conclusion from knowing how much was spent is there the kind of "subordinating" interest which would justify governmental monitoring for the first time of efforts to influence public opinion.

The Supreme Court has never permitted government regulation of such indirect efforts to influence the legislative or elective process. Decisions of the present Court, as well as a long line of earlier cases over a twenty-year period, make it quite clear that the Court would strike down such a broad congressional effort to have the government monitor lobbying solicitations.

In *United States* v. *Rumely*,[31] the Court considered the scope of the authority of the House Select Committee on Lobbying Activities to investigate the adequacy of the Lobbying Regulation Act. One group under investigation refused to comply with a committee subpoena seeking disclosure of bulk purchasers of their books. In the words of the committee, the group's purpose was "distribution of printed material to influence legislation indirectly." To avoid raising serious constitutional questions, the Court drastically narrowed the scope of the House investigation on the ground that:

> [T]he power to inquire into all efforts of private individuals to influence public opinion through books and periodicals, however remote the radiations of influence which they may exert upon the ultimate legislative process, raises doubts of the constitutionality in view of the prohibitions of the First Amendment.[32]

The Supreme Court limited the investigation to " 'representations made directly to the Congress, its members, or its Committees.' "[33]

One year later, the Supreme Court, in *United States* v. *Harriss*,[34] applied the same construction to the language of the Federal Regulation of Lobbying Act itself. Several persons had been indicted under the act for failure to report expenditures related "to the costs of a

---

[31] 345 U.S. 41 (1953).

[32] Ibid., p. 46.

[33] Ibid., p. 47.

[34] 347 U.S. 612.

campaign to communicate by letter with members of Congress on certain legislation."[35] The Court took care not "to deny Congress in large measure the power of self-protection" by preventing Congress from any regulation of lobbying.[36] But, as in *Rumely*, Chief Justice Warren limited the reach of the act to " 'lobbying in its commonly accepted sense'—to direct communication with members of Congress on pending or proposed Federal legislation."[37]

The Supreme Court has not faced the issue of lobbying since the *Harriss* decision. However, there is every reason to believe the Court would adopt the same analysis today.

In the sections of *Buckley* v. *Valeo*[38] concerning the disclosure of political contributions and expenditures, the Supreme Court dealt with analogous issues. Said the Court, ". . . we have repeatedly found that compelled disclosure, in itself, can seriously infringe on privacy of association and belief guaranteed by the First Amendment."[39] The Court held that governmental interests supporting disclosure— informing the public about the sources and uses of political money, thereby helping to eliminate corruption—were strong enough to validate such requirements for political committees controlled by candidates.

But, when it came to independent political committees and individuals, the Court made an important distinction. Applying a First Amendment analysis, it said such independent efforts have to be disclosed *only* if the major purpose of those efforts is to nominate or elect candidates, and *only* if they involve communications that in express terms "advocate the election or defeat of a clearly identified candidate."[40] Other independent expenditures, those which do not explicitly advocate election or defeat of a candidate, do not fall within "the core area sought to be addressed by Congress"[41] and thus Congress cannot require their disclosure.

In narrowly construing the definitions of political campaign expenditures, the Court adopted the same position that had led the Court of Appeals to strike down broader disclosure provisions of the Federal Election Campaign Act (FECA). That portion of the decision was not appealed to the Supreme Court.

---

[35] Ibid., p. 615.

[36] Ibid., p. 625.

[37] Ibid., p. 620.

[38] 424 U.S. 1.

[39] Ibid., p. 64.

[40] Ibid., p. 80.

[41] Ibid., p. 79.

Section 308 of the FECA required disclosure by any group that committed "any act directed to the public for the purpose of influencing the outcome of an election or publication or broadcast of any material that is designed to influence individuals to cast their votes for or against such candidate or to withhold their votes from such candidate."[42]

The section was held flatly unconstitutional by the Court of Appeals. The Court cited the Second Circuit opinion in *United States v. National Committee for Impeachment*.[43] In that case, the United States Court of Appeals for the Second Circuit narrowly construed the section of the 1971 FECA requiring disclosure of activities aimed at the public by political committees. The Second Circuit said a broader reading of this section would result in an enormous interception of activities protected by the First Amendment:

> [E]very position on any issue, major or minor, taken by anyone would be a campaign issue and any comment upon it, in, say a newspaper editorial or an advertisement, would be subject to proscription unless the registration and disclosure were complied with. Such a result would, we think, be abhorrent; . . . Any organization would be wary of expressing any view-point lest under the Act it be required to register, file reports, disclose its contributors, or the like. On the Government's thesis every little Audubon Society Chapter would be a "political committee" for "environment" is an issue in one campaign after another. On this basis, too, a Boy Scout troop advertising for membership to combat "juvenile delinquency" or a Golden Age Club promoting "senior citizens rights" would fall under the Act. The dampening effect on First Amendment rights and the potential for arbitrary administrative action that would result from such a situation would be intolerable.[44]

Supporters of coverage of "grass-roots" lobbying solicitation argue that a member of Congress needs to know who "stimulated" the writing of the letters they receive in order to evaluate the intensity of the views of the writers. There is often a suggestion[45] that the

---

[42] Buckley v. Valeo, 519 F.2d 821, 870 (D.C. Cir. 1975).

[43] 469 F.2d 1135 (2nd Cir. 1972).

[44] 469 F.2d 1135, 1142. Similarly, in ACLU v. Jennings, 336 F. Supp. 1941 (D.D.C. 1975), *vacated as moot sub nom.*, Staats v. ACLU, 422 U.S. 1030 (1975), a three-judge district court was faced with a challenge to the 1971 FECA. The court perceived the same constitutional obstacles and adopted the same narrow interpretation propounded in *National Committee for Impeachment*.

[45] See comments of Senator Ribicoff, above, at p. 16.

letters are somehow less worthy of consideration if they are not spontaneous. The best response to this wholly erroneous argument can be found in the testimony of a representative of the American Automobile Association:

> This is an absurd test. My dictionary defines spontaneous as "happening or arising without apparent external cause . . . unpremeditated . . . unconstrained and unstudied in manner or behavior." In other words, a communication from someone who had not studied the issues or was scarcely aware of them would be more valued than one from someone who did know what he was talking about under this criteria.
>
> And where would the latter gain his information? In most cases, not from the commercial mass media which simply does not have the space (in the case of publications) or the time (in the case of television and radio) to cover all the issues that interest all of the nation's diverse groups and individuals. . . . The answer is through special committees, ad hoc groups and voluntary citizen's organizations often set up to deal with one specific issue.[46]

Applying the *Buckley* standard to government monitoring of grass-roots lobbying, the conclusion is inescapable that for most such activities there is not even a legitimate, much less a subordinating, interest.

Only two circumstances present even an arguably subordinating governmental interest in lobbying solicitation: first, where extremely large sums of money (hundreds of thousands of dollars) are spent on a particular issue, and, second, where an organization solicits lobbying by its own employees or by other individuals or organizations subject to economic pressure by the lobbying organization. Where the soliciting organization is simply serving as a conduit for information, no disclosure is necessary or justifiable unless the amounts it spends are so vast that the Congress and the public should be alerted to the intensity of the lobbyists' interest.

Contributors

When lobbying reform began in the 94th Congress, reform advocates sought the public disclosure of all contributors to any lobbying organization. Increasingly, members of Congress have come to appreciate

---

[46] Statement of John deLorenzi, American Automobile Association, before the Subcommittee on Administrative Law and Governmental Relations, House Committee on the Judiciary, April 6, 1977.

the First Amendment infringements associated with this issue. As indicated above, all of the bills now attempt to protect the small contributor from disclosure. In approving H.R. 8494, the House subcommittee, by a narrow vote, deleted any requirement for disclosure of contributions. S. 1785 would still require disclosure of contributions of above $3,000 to any organization which spends 1 percent of its budget on lobbying, no matter the size of the organization.

The primary interest of the reformers seems to be to identify those organizations which appear to be broad-based citizens' groups but are really entirely funded by a select group of corporations or individuals attempting to hide their "special interest" in a cloak of "public interest." The other goal seems to be to identify any contributors who, because of the amounts of money they give, have a very high degree of control over an organization's activities.

The First Amendment interests invaded here are twofold. First, anonymous political speech is part of our First Amendment heritage. Protecting the right to seek to influence public affairs without having to sacrifice one's anonymity is important to encourage the presentation of new, unorthodox, or unpopular views. In the words of the Supreme Court:

> Anonymous pamphlets, leaflets, brochures, and even books have played an important role in the progress of mankind. Persecuted groups and sects from time to time throughout history have been able to criticize oppressive practices and laws either anonymously or not at all. . . . Even the Federalist Papers, written in favor of the adoption of our Constitution, were published under fictitious names. It is plain that anonymity has sometimes been assumed for the most constructive purposes.[47]

Second, where there is a possibility of reprisal, the Supreme Court has mandated a special right to keep members and contributors secret. The Supreme Court first recognized this right of associational privacy in *NAACP* v. *Alabama ex rel. Patterson*.[48] There, it unanimously reversed a contempt conviction for failure to disclose the membership list of the NAACP, on the theory that the inviolability of privacy in group associations may be indispensable to the preservation of freedom of association.

The holding of *NAACP* v. *Alabama* was affirmed in several subsequent cases. In *Bates* v. *Little Rock*,[49] the Supreme Court unani-

---

[47] Talley v. California, 362 U.S. 60, 64-65 (1960).
[48] 357 U.S. 449 (1958).
[49] 361 U.S. 516 (1960).

mously invalidated a conviction based on the refusal of the NAACP to furnish city tax officials with membership lists. In *Louisiana ex rel. Gremillion v. NAACP*,[50] the Supreme Court unanimously affirmed a lower court decision enjoining the enforcement of a statute requiring the disclosure of membership lists of the local NAACP.[51]

The principle of the NAACP cases has been applied to other situations. In *Shelton v. Tucker*,[52] the Court invalidated an Arkansas statute which compelled teachers to disclose all of their organizational affiliations for the past five years. And in *Talley v. California*,[53] the Court ruled unconstitutional "on its face" a Los Angeles ordinance prohibiting the anonymous distribution of any handbill.

The Supreme Court in *Buckley* cited these cases with approval in invalidating disclosure of members of independent committees, clearly indicating it would not tolerate a contributor disclosure statute that affected the funding of every conceivable general interest organization engaged in political activities. Said the Court: "When it is an individual other than a candidate or a group other than a 'political committee' the relation of the information sought to the purposes of the Act may be too remote."[54]

In addition, in the context of the First Amendment, the Supreme Court has imposed the additional requirement of "less drastic means." The Court wrote in *Shelton v. Tucker* that

> even though the governmental purpose be legitimate and substantial, that purpose cannot be pursued by means that stifle fundamental personal liberties when the end can be more narrowly achieved. The breadth of legislative abridgement must be viewed in the light of less drastic means for achieving the same basic purpose.[55]

And indeed the impact on individuals can be enormous. Contributors to lobbying organizations must either face public disclosure of their support or withhold their contributions. For many citizens this may be their only means of participating in the organization. It may be the only way they express their views. For those individuals

---

[50] 366 U.S. 293 (1961).

[51] See also Gibson v. Florida Legislative Investigation Committee, 372 U.S. 539 (1963). In *Gibson*, the Supreme Court suggested that it would approve membership list disclosure only where there was a very specific and formal investigation of criminal subversive activity, as in the Communist party case. Communist Party v. Subversive Activities Control Board, 367 U.S. 1 (1961).

[52] 364 U.S. 479 (1960).

[53] 362 U.S. 60 (1960).

[54] 429 U.S. 79, 80.

[55] 364 U.S. 479, 488 (1960).

involved with unpopular causes, the deterrent is great. A contributor to conservative causes can be fired if his or her name is discovered on a lobbying report by a liberal employer. An employer who supports the broad availability of abortion may retaliate against employees who lobby to restrict it. The examples are endless. And organizations required to disclose their contributors will, as a result, find fund raising more difficult and presentation of their views less possible.

The contributor disclosure provisions of the bills which would still require some disclosure clearly do not meet this test or the one set out in *Buckley*. In most organizations those who contribute $2,500 or $3,000 could not in any sense control the organization. Also, where there are many contributors, the likelihood that it is a "shell" for secret special interests is remote. Congress is required to identify the point at which these inferences of influence or deception can be drawn. So far they have not done so.

Enforcement

One of the chief arguments for lobbying law reform is the almost total lack of enforcement of the existing law. Under the 1946 law, reports are filed with the clerk of the House and the secretary of the Senate and are printed in the *Congressional Record*.[56] The only penalties for noncompliance are criminal. They have rarely been invoked.[57] A 1975 report by the General Accounting Office concluded:

> Although the Clerk of the House and the Secretary of the Senate have responsibility for administering the Act, they do not have the investigative authority, the right to inspect records, or enforcement power. . . . [T]he Act does not specifically authorize Justice to monitor lobbying activities.[58]

And in their 1977 testimony, both the deputy attorney general and the deputy comptroller general echoed these conclusions.[59]

---

[56] Section 308(b), Legislative Reorganization Act, 60 Stat. 812, 839 (1946).

[57] The Justice Department in 1968 could only identify five cases involving the act, one of which was the *Harriss* case. Congressional Quarterly, *Legislators and the Lobbyists*, 2nd ed. (Washington, D.C., May 1968), p. 13.

[58] Comptroller General, "The Federal Regulation of Lobbying Act—Difficulties in Enforcement and Administration," April 2, 1975, in House *Hearings on Public Disclosure of Lobbying Act*, September 12, 1975, p. 692.

[59] Testimony of Peter F. Flaherty, deputy attorney general, before the Subcommittee on Administrative Law and Governmental Relations, House Committee on the Judiciary, April 21, 1977; testimony of Robert F. Keller, deputy comptroller general, April 6, 1977.

All of the bills are similar in their grant of enforcement powers. All authorize the comptroller general to require by subpoena submission of "such reports, records, correspondence," and answers to questions the comptroller general "may consider necessary to carry out provisions of this Act." All authorize the comptroller general to issue advisory opinions and to carry out investigations of possible violations. The attorney general is empowered to seek to enjoin conduct which violates the law, presumably including the power to halt lobbying in the absence of registration or adequate reporting. The attorney general is also responsible for prosecuting criminal offenses under the bills.

The bills have never contained any detailed scheme to govern the conduct of the comptroller general. There are no restrictions at all on the attorney general. A general provision in all of the bills requiring that investigations be conducted "with due regard for the rights and privacy" of the individual or organization involved contains no specifics. H.R. 5578 is the only bill which bars the comptroller general from access to membership or contributor lists of voluntary membership organizations as an exercise of the enforcement powers given by the bill. Only H.R. 5795 was introduced in a form even slightly sensitive to the problem. It subjected the actions of the comptroller general to the requirements of the Administrative Procedure Act, the Freedom of Information Act, and the Privacy Act. Both H.R. 8494 and S. 1785 now at least contain this same provision.

Despite the sweeping authority which would be conferred by these provisions, they have received little close attention. For many members of Congress and witnesses who have testified on the bills, they have been relatively uncontroversial. By and large, the alarms raised by some have been ignored. To a Congress that has already created the Federal Election Commission with its broad monitoring responsibility over campaign finance, these bills may seem only a small and logical next step. However, to give the government a broad arsenal of weapons with which to monitor lobbying could be very dangerous. As one commentator has observed, a government agency "charged with the *regulation of politics* is an extraordinary assault on First Amendment rights in political democracy."[60] In the words of another, "Getting elected has become a regulated industry."[61] Yet, despite the grant of broad enforcement powers, no one has really

---

[60] Lipow, "Political Reform as a Danger to Democracy," p. 269.

[61] Remarks of Ronald Eastman, general counsel, Democratic National Committee, "Lawyers in Politics," Virginia Bar Association Panel, The Greenbrier, White Sulphur Springs, West Virginia, July 15, 1977.

focused on whether we want advocacy of legislative change to become yet another such industry.

Where First Amendment interests are at stake, the Supreme Court has ruled repeatedly that excessive discretion is unconstitutional.[62] With thresholds low enough to sweep in thousands of small business and citizens' groups doing essentially intermittent or low-budget lobbying, the flood of paper will drown the comptroller general unless he or she picks and chooses targets for investigation. The bills establish no criteria for such investigations and leave the comptroller general total discretion. A corrupt or overzealous person could use these powers to harass enemies, to deter one side in a controversial legislative battle, or to do a staggering number of other improper things. Having just come through the Watergate era, the public cannot be asked to trust government officials to use such broad power over political activity wisely and well.

These fears are not merely speculative. According to a recent report, it took the Federal Election Commission approximately thirty-five person-years in 1976 to audit just the reports of the fifteen candidates who received matching funds during the presidential primaries.[63] There is no way that the comptroller general will have adequate resources to monitor everyone. Experience in California provides evidence of discretion in actual operation. The Lipow study on California's Proposition 9 reported:

> Given the liberal leanings of the staff and the chief officials of the Commission at the present time (both were officials of California Rural Legal Services), it is not surprising that the first group which came to the FPPC's notice and was required to file was Gallo Winery.[64]

Enforcement programs which permit this kind of selective enforcement must be limited by legislative standards. Criteria for opening investigations and a procedure whereby a group under investigation can raise and have considered the question of selective investigation on improper grounds are needed.

The power to demand more information as an adjunct to en-

---

[62] See discussion in Brice Clagett and John Bolton, "Buckley v. Valeo, Its Aftermath, and Its Prospects: The Constitutionality of Government Restraints on Political Campaign Financing," *Vanderbilt Law Review*, vol. 29 (November 1976), p. 1327, 1358-60.

[63] Michael J. Malbin, "After Surviving Its First Election Year, FEC is Wary of the Future," *National Journal*, vol. 469 (March 26, 1977).

[64] Lipow, "Political Reform and the Regulation of Lobbying: The California Experience after Two Years," p. 15.

forcing the reporting requirements can also be a dangerous weapon. Again, California provides us with real examples. The California Franchise Tax Board, in auditing statements for the California Fair Political Practices Commission (FPPC) has subpoenaed the records of the Northern California Civil Liberties Union, which refused an open-ended informal request for all its records on lobbying. The subpoena of the Franchise Tax Board sought an extraordinary amount of detailed internal information. Among other documents, it sought records of all cash receipts and disbursements, bank statements, deposit slips, cancelled checks, petty cash records, credit card statements and supporting vouchers, professional diaries, appointment calendars, and correspondence with state officials. The FTB also sought to question the organization's employees about the activities of its lobbyists.[65] On May 26, 1976, the FTB filed suit in the California courts to compel compliance with the subpoena.[66]

In another case, a young woman lobbyist for the Friends Committee on Legislation made her living room couch available to a friend of hers, a young woman consultant to a joint committee of the legislature. The consultant lived 150 miles from Sacramento, had worked late that night, and had to be in a committee hearing early the next morning. In an excess of caution, the Friends' lobbyist listed the loan of the couch as a "gift" to the consultant. At the time of her field audit, the auditor demanded that she provide him with an exact value of a night's sleep on the couch.[67]

Methods of investigation present yet another problem. Presumably the comptroller general will employ investigators. Armed with a congressional mandate to investigate lobbying, investigators will be unrestrained by the lobbying statute in their use of a wide variety of "political surveillance" techniques such as compiling files on groups engaged in lobbying and on politicians meeting with lobbyists, using informers, wiretaps, and other questionable investigative techniques. After a decade of disclosures of government political surveillance, we need to write specific prohibitions into the legislation to circumscribe the zeal of investigators with both bad and good intentions.

---

[65] Interview with Charles Marson, legal director, ACLU of Northern California, May 27, 1977.
[66] Petition for Order to Produce Books and Records, *In the Matter of the Audit of the Franchise Tax Board*, No. 723-548 (Calif. Superior Court, S.F. May 26, 1977).
[67] Letter from Brent A. Barnhart, legislative counsel, ACLU of Northern California, July 6, 1977.

A warning, too, must be issued about the use by other government officials of all of the information gathered by the comptroller general. Two of the bills would put private lobbying efforts at a tremendous disadvantage vis-à-vis government lobbyists, who would be freed from all disclosure requirements. There is little likelihood that they will ever be treated as lobbyists as these bills are considered. Yet there is no limit in any of the bills on their access to information collected on covered lobbyists, whether public or not. Government lobbyists will be able to obtain their adversaries' priorities, directions, capacities, and operations without having to disclose anything. Moreover, virtually no sanctions have been written in to prevent what all would agree were improper uses of this information. In this connection, it is well to remember that the "enemies list" was compiled in large part from lists of contributors to Democratic candidates.[68]

---

[68] Ralph K. Winter, Jr., *Watergate and the Law* (Washington, D.C.: American Enterprise Institute, 1974), p. 28, footnote 54.

5
CONCLUSION

Congress seeks to remedy abuses, through lobbying reform, but the drafters have failed to keep those abuses firmly in mind when actually preparing legislation. With a few exceptions, the bills include within their reach many groups and individuals whose lobbying activities contain no potential for abuse. When the First Amendment is at stake, such broad disclosure cannot be justified and will not be useful. As in California, a "blizzard of paper" will produce a "disenchanted yawn from the public." In contrast, lobbying disclosure which focused on only the largest efforts might provide Congress and the public with the kind of "early warning" system they seek.

The Congress appears to have been unduly influenced by the lobbyists' ugly image. As V. O. Key has put it, "The view that pressure groups are pathological growth in the body politic is likewise more picturesque than accurate."[1] The Congress would do well to try to distinguish fact from fantasy. A good way to begin would be by paying more than lip service to the fact that lobbying is indeed that First Amendment right to petition for redress of grievances.

---

[1] Key, *Politics, Parties and Pressure Groups*, p. 130.

Cover and book design: Pat Taylor